SUMMONED

Also by Margaret Hasse

Stars Above, Stars Below

In a Sheep's Eye, Darling

Milk and Tides

Earth's Appetite

Between Us

A Little Book of Abundance (editor)

Rocked by the Waters: Poems of Motherhood
(co-editor with poet Athena Kildegaard)

Shelter (collaborator
with visual artist Sharon DeMark)

SUMMONED

poems

Margaret Hasse

NODIN PRESS

Acknowledgements

"Passing Storm" and "Spring Aubade in Blue" were written as part of the 2021 Dick Scuglik Memorial Residency and Scholarship to encourage ekphrastic writing, a project of Write On, Door County. Guest Editor Aliki Barnstone chose "During the Long Stay-at-Home" for the winter 2021 issue of *Persimmon Tree*. "Summer of Love, 1967" appears in the 2018 anthology, *Visiting Bob: Poems Inspired by the Life and Work of Bob Dylan*. "Night on the Town" and "Red Dress" were each winners in annual poetry contests sponsored by Common Good Books and published on the store's website.

Cover photograph and book design by John Toren.

ISBN: 978-1-947237-38-4

9 8 7 6 5 4 3 2 1

Library of Congress Control Number: 2021946696

Published by
Nodin Press
5114 Cedar Lake Road
Minneapolis, MN   55416

Printed in U.S.A.

Summoned is a work of memory and imagination. The incidents, characters, and dialogue are not to be construed as factual.

For mothers and sons,
and my mother and my sons

CONTENTS

ONE

TWO

THREE

In the silence between your heartbeats bides
a summons. Do you hear it? Name it if you must,
or leave it forever nameless, but why pretend
it is not there?

—Jalāl ad-Dīn Muḥammad Rūmī

ONE

BORN INTO ONE BODY

Isn't it odd how we're born
in one country
and not another,
could have been any other
color instead of what
we are? We might speak
Parsi and send our dead
to the place of birds.
Strange that we work
at desks in cool rooms
not making clothes
in factories, sweltering,
being slapped or called
Donkey or *Dog*.

What if we suddenly changed
into another, disappeared
into a labyrinthine souk,
wearing shorts and
a baseball cap, emerging
as a man in a djellaba
or a woman with red
embroidery of henna
on her hands?
We'd sit in the shade
of a palm tree, feed dates
to a child never seen before
but surely she is ours.

TRAVELER AWAKE AT NIGHT

Stripped down to a body, suitcase, car, miles along,
you don't know who or where you are, only that
you're in a room and have a heart juttering inside
its bony cage. Nearby something is shoving
a loose branch or pry bar against sideboards.
Silence and again sound, so that your eyes open
as you decide whether the beats are regular
or uneven and whether to get up, grope toward
the square of gray window, peer out to learn
wind is the only visitor.

You're not yourself yet, whoever
that might be, but appear to be someone comfortable
with not knowing. As if meeting yourself as a baby,
you count fingers, move toes; your tongue prowls
the mouth to find customary rough spots on a tooth.
Thud: that noise again. In the meandering current
of farawayness, you drift in a bed smelling slightly
of cloves, study shadows of furniture you didn't buy.

Without a schedule, calendar, without familiars,
not people, books, maps or mentors, a trail
of personal history, you're suspended, a clear drop
of water that grows pendulous and falls free.

LEMON AND LAMB

Preserved lemon on a plate of couscous
makes me think of a lamb
in Morocco turning on a spit in the dusty heat.
A boy with a flyswatter whipped the air.
This was north of the Atlas Mountains
where I saw monkeys in the wild
more aggressive than beggars.

Traveling the way I did was work—
staying at the cheapest places,
one meal a day so money would last.
This was the way I could afford the world.

As a girl I fed lambs from baby bottles.
One sucked so hard the rubber nipple
failed and a splat of milk wetted its face.
With long bleats, the lamb uttered
its hunger and confusion.
I saw lambs excited, sad, disappointed—
never would I eat any part of them
until the day I learned what hunger can do.

IT RAINED IN PARIS

the kind of rain that came
       from clouds behind
              the Eiffel Tower scuttling in
                     to shower a dark April all day
                            on red geraniums in window boxes.

I walked along a rue in damp shoes,
       homesick tears disguised as rain.
              Strangers carried their weather
                     beneath umbrellas as if in
                            separate planetary systems.

Slim women were embraced
       by trench coats with wide belts.
              Drizzle bedraggled the hem
                     of my skirt making me
                            unfashionable as a scullery maid.

The cold rain persisted.
       Inside a patisserie, trays
              of crescent rolls just baked.
                     At a table beside a window
                            I tasted a croissant for the first time.

Flakes from its golden dome,
       buttery layers of pastry
              to savor, and no one hurried
                     while dazzling sheets
                            of rain continued to fall in Paris.

ANOTHER DAY OF BEING WHITE
[AT SELBY AND DALE]

near midnight with Willie
a.k.a. Opio out of jail just months
between his nickel and his dime.
I had wheels; he was broke,
directed me where his daddy was
for maybe money maybe dope
in a basement down a staircase
to a hidey-hole where dice and cups
slammed and Black men's voices
bounced and rattled like ice
in a blender, a clatter of speech
jive and hotshot fast,
nothing I could understand
when I entered the basement room
except their maleness
meteoric in a black box.

The sheet of sound tore
as every man turned a moment
of silence to size us up—not cops
just old Senior's son Willie
with a pale hippie chick—
long hair, long skirt, forgettable
like an ad for plain white rice.
The men blended back
into their game like a swirl
of what I thought but
shouldn't say—*smoke*—
except one older man who
slipped something to Willie,

turned to me saying softly:
This is no place for you.
Now begone.

SUMMER OF LOVE, 1967

Some men she picked up at a rally
or rock concert called her Earth Mother.
She'd be wearing a peasant blouse
and he'd have a peace sign on his T-shirt,
torn jeans pinned at the zipper.
His mouth tasted of garlic hummus.
Her perfume was patchouli oil.
On his *Nashville Skyline* album,
Dylan kept singing "Lay, lady, lay
Lay across my big brass bed."

A lover with magical powers
taught her positions she'd never
heard of until *The Joy of Sex*.
Sometimes they made love
in an apartment with beaded curtains,
candles in Chianti bottles
or on a yoga mat where mung beans
in the kitchen were beginning to sprout.
Once in a hammock and once, just once,
in a big brass bed.

MARIJUANA

When I placed a bag filled
with marijuana candy on the porch
for my friend Patsy to pick up
on a solemn mission,
Alice B. Toklas came to mind—
college kids in the '60s favored
her recipe for marijuana fudge.

Back then hot seeds from joints left
holes in the cotton shirts of boys
in my newly co-ed dorm.
I preferred to eat grass rather than smoke it
to avoid a burning throat,
an illicit scent in my hair.

No one could predict who
would get swept away by drugs and alcohol,
lost and addicted most of their lives.

Fifty years later on a vacation in Colorado
I surprised myself and my husband
by wanting to see inside a cannabis shop
where I bought gummy bears, *enhanced*.

I told Patsy about my purchase
hidden in the medicine cabinet, then
forgotten until tonight when she phoned
to tell me Jay's death nears.
Oxycodone makes him sleep away
his last nights and days, marijuana
might ease pain's grip, let him be
present for the time he has.
Yes, I still had some to share.

LIAR

A fib slipped from his mouth, his wife knew
by the smell of its bad breath.
It was a guppy of a falsehood
about the time he returned home
and what an expense was for.
She put the little squirmer in a jar
of water where it swam in circles.

The next week the man spit out a smelt,
then a skinny pike too small to fry.
She bought an aquarium and glass pirate
with one eye to blow bubbles from the bottom.
Dandruff of fish food floated on top.

Her husband released 14-karat coins
of goldfish and an astounding neon tetra
visible in the black waters of night.
When the tank greened up, smelled rank,
she housed the fish in waxy
take-out cartons from a Chinese restaurant,
then scrubbed the container clean.

The final lie that fell from her husband's lips
was a shark ballooning to full size
on the living room carpet.
Its teeth latched onto the man's ankle like a metal trap.
Finally free to escape, she released the hook
from her lips and slipped out the door
into buoyant air.

A MOTEL IN CUSTER, SOUTH DAKOTA

Moths big as hands wave
over a window box at dusk.

On a billboard down the street
General George, hair golden and long
as a girl's, sits on his horse Comanche.
Words bubble from his mouth:
Beautiful Black Hills!
Shore wish I'd stayed.

Thirty years ago you strode out
of the bar and rode off on your motorcycle,
a yahoo drunk who couldn't be stopped
until the road by the Needles curved.
I'm sick of willful men, men
who seek danger and war.

The silent moon ascends:
an angel, a bird, a flower.

ANOTHER DAY OF BEING WHITE
[IN SOUTH DAKOTA]

My husband ambles into the kitchen
to help with the stew—
its plenty of meat and fresh beans.
I say I have *Indians* on my hands
when I meant *onions*. My eyes water
with the odor of white rings
around my fingers or maybe
I'm crying because the two dollars
I gave to the worn-down man
with his cardboard sign was almost nothing.

Feelings churn and I mistake words
as if on laughing gas
given to a woman with a broken tooth
who could afford pain-free repair.
My friend Roy said gaps and stubs
of tattletale teeth tell of someone
growing up poor.
He smiled with his mouth closed.

My tongue slipped onto *Indians*
because deep into the night
I'd read a book about Wounded Knee
then attended a workshop
about the trauma of being white,
how we carry in our bodies
collective *quilt*, I mean *guilt*.

I twirl a confirmation ring
on my finger, its rose gold

grape leaves from a mine
in the Black Hills where
prospectors trampled treaties
making it possible 70 years later
for my family to build
a house on South Dakota soil
in a land grab we didn't want
to see. Sometimes my mother
sent money to Pine Ridge Reservation
along with secondhand clothes.

ANOTHER DAY OF BEING WHITE
[DOG INCIDENT REPORT]

My goldendoodle puppy, apricot-colored,
looks like a dust mop on legs.
Rosie adores everyone, wants to lick hands,
is friendly indiscriminately with all humans
in her orbit, lucky little star, recipient
of sunny attention from many strangers
until today when I errored (as the training book
calls it), let out the leash five feet
and unheeded her dash through the doorway
of a bus shelter where a man sat
slumped smoking a cigarette.
When she came at him, he leaped to his feet,
onto the bench the way fire jumps,
his dark eyes on her, his face a rictus of terror.
Was he yanked back to facing a mouthful
of guard dogs' teeth? Or to a traffic stop
with K-9 cops who call Black men *dog biscuits*?
Maybe he's been warned of feral dogs and rabies.
Need I tell you I'm a white woman
in a mostly white neighborhood,
and like the puppy, I'm used to being liked?
He is a Black man uninterested in the apology
I try to make from a distance. Am I wrong
to make this encounter about race?
Can he just be a guy with a primal fear of dogs?

MILKY WAY

Sometimes up north the scent
of wildness in the cold woods
makes her turn back to rooms
for the comfort of fire and food.

What happened to the fearless girl
wearing her father's great coat of wool
who liked to walk in the dark?

On clear winter nights she'd stretch out
on a snowy field to wander the sky
searching for Cassiopeia atop
the Milky Way, and Aquarius,
cup-bearing acquaintance of youth.

She'd shout out to Orion, intrepid
hunter, and provide the little bear
a cloud cover with an exhalation of breath.

We each have a polestar to guide us
that is our grieving wound,
our healing friend. When we're alone,
it can rise in us as origin and map.

RUMINATIONS ON BELIEF IN A HIGHER POWER

Watching an old woman in her babushka
bend on her knees to the statue of Jesus
that Tilman Riemenschneider carved
from worm-worn wood is to admire
an act of faith and want to emulate it.
Some bow simply to the beauty of the art.

Even if we don't believe, we are invited to act
as if. As if our god, personal as a parent,
sticks stars like insistent and friendly fireflies
in the night sky for us. As if there is a reason
millions of people go hungry, a purpose
for cancer in Rose's blood.

Every sentient being finds confidence
in a deity difficult when the nightly news
features so much hardship and death.
We remain bewildered that the small girls
in the house fire will never return
to their dining room table where they nibbled corn,
their teeth small and secretive as rabbits'.
And how can those babies with globular heads
and extra limbs on display in bottles
at the Mütter Museum offer anything but disbelief?

Marianne, 20 years sober, says she draws
a happy face on her calendar every day
to remind herself to trust the design
of a higher power and help her
keep the cork in the bottle.
A speaker proposes reincarnation as a twist
on the idea of suffering. He advises praying

that our next life, preferably brief, is one
of intense anguish that pays for the right to rise
toward the goodness a holy being desires for us
like a diamond from the slag,
pressured and heated to become
clear and beautiful as a soul.

As the saying goes, we sail under sealed orders.
Even though many days seem ruled
not by a moral lodestar, but by a sulfuric devil
or a wild and fickle Zeus prone to hurling
thunderbolts or turning women into cows,
let's assume the existence of a god or goddess
with secret long-range plans. Living as if
a heavenly force will judge us later
may make us better people—
and create a better world right now.

BUTTERFLY, MY FRIEND

If I say the heart is a butterfly,
its wings easily torn by hard touch,
would that explain this summer
when the least wind scatters intentions
like blown seeds and the brevity of life
is everywhere evident?

At night, a daylily withdraws its bloom.
Around the clock, forests flame in Oregon.
Gunfire's reported near the Floyd memorial.

My friend and I were born
on the same cold day in February.
On our last birthday, he proclaimed
us littermates   he, whose
sudden death bent my internal compass.
I don't always know what day it is.
Even the sun seems off, a sick orange
in the smoke-sodden sky.

How to carry the heaviness
of someone forever absent?
On papery wings a white butterfly
flutters through the haze.

GRASSHOPPER

Today the air smells of heated grain.
She and her daughter stand by the barn. Already
autumn is a place between anticipation and fear.
The dry fields are full of grasshoppers.
They display confidence in daylight.
Propelled by their hind legs, they take off
with a whirr of wings through the high grasses.
In the fable, a grasshopper's the improvident one,
nothing to eat come winter, which seems just.
Where swarms darken the skies, everything is
devoured—harvest, broom straw, doll's hair.
Nearby, corn plants spout tassels,
soybeans dangle green pods.

A grasshopper captured in a hand
will spit tobacco brown. While she holds it,
time spools out on the threshold
of ingathering, of having or losing yield
before it's secured. It is so in the Great Plains
as it is in Kenya and Ethiopia, as it has been across time,
the bending of human livelihood to the unpredictable.
She releases the grasshopper. It jumps
onto her daughter's head, attaching
like a barrette to a wave of hair.
All around is green and brown and gold.

—*After Eavan Boland's "Moth"*

30

SAINT FRANCIS PET CEMETERY

Under our dog's tongue
the stone of a tumor.
We always fed her dry food
but now offer a death row diet,
whatever the pooch wants:
meat scraps from our plates,
casserole with rice.

We walk slowly, let her go
unleashed, stopping in a pet cemetery.
A granite statue of Saint Francis
stands watch over the tombstones.
He who tamed the wolf
believed in the souls of animals.
He raises his hand to bless them all.

We'll be back soon to plant ashes
among the grave markers remembering
Teensy, a terrier, Busy Bob, a hamster,
and on a cross made of Popsicle sticks:
Spaz the guppy, swimming forever.

BY THE LAKE IN THE LATE HOURS

The moon hangs,
a slim white clip
in the black hair of night.
The sky is scratched
by its castoff burnings.
Not enough light
in moon and meteors
to see my feet step onto the dock,
which rocks softly.
I shift my weight
to balance upright.
A bullfrog sounds
like a cello being played
with a broken-stringed bow.
Imperfection doesn't bother me.
Sometimes we try too hard.
I don't want anything more
except to lie down
on the wooden boards,
watch the light show
and listen to reeds
whisper in the dark.

MY MOOSE

A mossy boulder rose from the lake.
Water poured from its back
and shoulders, taking massive shape.
A moose waded into the shallows
of green water,
his face like a shovel of coal.

Nothing rushed his majesty, my moose,
not tourists' chatter
on walkways, cameras snapping,
not plop of turtles launching
from lily pads.
As if alone in the world,
the moose did not turn his head,
stepped onto shore.

Everything grew silent as he passed
through tamarack and scrub pines,
disappeared toward deeper forest.

Over the years since that sighting,
when harassed by daily life,
unanswered requests, my shortcomings,
I remember the dignity of the moose,
how he moved like a god who knew
the weight of his antlers
not as weapons, but worthiness.

TWO

BEHOLD DECEMBER

To be held, the minister says, *we must behold.* Tonight
I behold a fringe of frost on the windows where
candlelight stutters. Although weary, I drive through
the dim evening to visit a friend who has fallen on ice.
I behold the winter's dark coming and the fear of being
brittle-boned and alone.

On my friend's kitchen counter squat numerous glass
bottles and jars—containers, she tells me, from cleaning
out her fridge, items past their expiration dates. *I hope
we last past our shelf life*, I joke, and we grin. With no
garbage disposal and no dishwasher, my friend lacks
the equipment to make it easy to scrub out the contents
and ready the glass for recycling.

Perhaps it was the kindness called for at church or what
I know as my attachment to order that prompts me
to swoop up a bag of her half-filled bottles and jars to clean
at my own house. At home I'm surprised to behold
my adult son around whom a confusing and smoky cloud
of alcohol and anger drifts. I stiffen in his presence.

But lo, he's eager to help, lifts the bag from my arms
like a baby. He twists tops off jars my arthritic hands
can't manage. He shakes red globs of ketchup into the sink.
We hover over the cauldron of a garbage disposal whirling
yellow chutney and fish sauce, rancid salad oil and green
peaches. We pinch our noses against the smell, laugh,
look outside where the lightest snow has begun to fall.

From a reflection in the window I behold:

Side by side
our shoulders touching
two animals yoked together.

ANOTHER DAY OF BEING WHITE
[SUMMONED]

One early morning with a few strangers—
white, Black, brown—I walk
in silence to the crossroads
where George Floyd died.

It's filled with balloons,
flowers woven into blankets,
stuffed bears, and among many,
this handmade sign:

All mothers were summoned
when George Floyd called out for his.

My thoughts are with my son,
who sizzles with fierce words,
not just for the policeman who
arrested him after curfew,
handcuffing him with zip ties.

He's also angry at me because
I adopted him or maybe because
I'm white like the cop and he is brown.
He refuses therapy, is moving out
in the middle of the pandemic
with no plans of where to live.

At home, in another shadowy dawn,
a family of crows argues.
Soon it will be light enough to see
how the maple hangs her head

over the grass.

I can't imagine the future for my son,
so I look backward to see
a small boy's beautiful body
walking into a swimming pool on tiptoe.
As the water gets deeper, he points
his nose up like a fox smelling the air.
He has always been audacious and brave—
it's something to hold onto.

GRIEF

Green tea in the night before first light.
It's early, even for me.
How to hold the day
in my arms like a day-old baby
struggling to survive,
her curled fingers tiny as wren's feet.
I dreamed my dog
smelled cancer in my throat.
I dreamed my son
was back in his room,
playing solitaire
and not in a jail cell alone,
his phone card spent.
I know how one hand holds the other
orbiting each knuckle with a thumb.
I'll do what I need to do.
I'll fall softly as light rain on myself.

POUCH

Small handprints of a child
marked the driveway's shoulder of wet sand
as if the breathing woods offered a sign
of his coming, the baby waiting weeks
for the agency to approve me as his mother.

It turned out that the impression
of palms and fingers
belonged to a possum on the night crew
that had cleared out mice, rotten apples, and slugs
from my garden and orchard.

Only once did I see her when an owl
called in the dark of the moon.
My flashlight's beam caught the little possum,
gray fur like a rat's,
her triangular face shaped like a party hat.
She backed away, a litter cozied
in the bulge of her marsupial pouch.

I would make my own pouch
to carry the little one when he arrived,
a suede sling lined with cotton to nestle
the baby, to hold him against my chest
and belly, my body a warming house.
My child would learn my heartbeat,
the intimate smell of me, hear songs
sung in a safe pocket of life.

PAINT FOR THE BABY'S ROOM

Tumbleweed, Ostrich Egg,
Algonquin—who dreams up
these names for paint on color strips,
labels, and formulas for mixing?

Who thinks of Homeland,
Cedar Chest, Alameda Red?
Of Raleigh Green, good for exteriors,
and Lemongrass for trim?

Poets! To name products
paint companies must hire those
who know the connotations of color,
who know how to be brief and stunning.

Water Mirror is light gray
like May rain or pencil tips.
The beige of Oatmeal Bath
works well with Upbeat Blue.

In a room of Yellow Water Lily,
a little boy lies in a crib.
He is the hue of Warm Earthenware
with a mouth of Deep Mulberry.

NOTES FROM A MOTHER'S DIARY

Awake with my one-track mind,
I used to hear the night train clack
through the city, my single wish:
want-a-child, want-a-child.

When my son arrived
through the channels of adoption,
the missing children on milk cartons
made me a thief.

When he was four I tell him more
about where he came from.
He knows babies are carried in the belly
so he thinks I ate him
like Pinocchio's whale.

Why was I in the hospital? Was I hurt?

No. Most babies are born in hospitals.
You were inside your first mother
ready to come out, first your head,
then the rest of your body.

He wants to talk about body parts.
He thinks my *bagina* is where pee comes from.

What are these bags on me called? he asks.
Testicles, I say.
What are your bumps here?
Nipples.
Did I drink from you?

I held you close and fed you from a bottle.

Where did I come from again?
he asked when he was six.
This time I pointed to my heart.
I will reach in and break it, he laughed.
Please wait, I say, *until you're older.*
I will ride a motorcycle, he threatened.
I will run away alone and—
(his boldest brag)—*I will pee on all your flowers.*

MOVING WATER

Before it fell, snow was water
and when captured in a warm mouth
it's water again. The image
of a child comes to mind
who did not live to be born
but is nearby in a pale storm
catching flakes in her mouth.
With her lips open like a fish
to unfulfilling air,
might she feel a momentary
cold glitter on her tongue
just as her name was held
briefly in our mouths?

Like a figure in the whiteout
of a blizzard, sometimes
she's here on earth
where my live-wire son
throws himself into life
like an Olympic diver into water
or an acrobat into air.
When he flings his body
backward onto a mattress
of snow, waving arms,
pumping legs to form
a snow angel who wears
a fan-like skirt, he calls
the shape *Lost Girl.*

I think of water on the move,
how snowfall in Minnesota

may have come
from the Mediterranean Sea
where a drop of water
could spend over 3,000 years
in the ocean before continuing
to another part of the cycle
from ice or snow to vapor and liquid.

I think of life on the move
from wish to beget, from ancestors
to me, to my children,
from an unborn daughter
to a living son, from breath
to death and carbon and stars.

ANOTHER DAY OF BEING WHITE
[WITH A NEIGHBOR WHO FORGETS
I'M A BLACK KID'S MOTHER]

A neighbor leans conspiratorially
out his car window to tell me
as I weed the boulevard:
There's a prowler around—
Black kid seen casing the alley,
taking pictures. Just warning you.

Acid in my throat almost burns
through superficial social skills
girls like me learned from mild
mothers who swallowed anger.
I say: *You're talking about my son.*

Were we wrong about the safety
of his summer job working
for the community council
that sends him with a camera
to find alley gardens worthy of awards?

RETURN OF THE SON

A bed made for guests
stands where a hand-me-down
crib used to be.
On a warm summer night
I enter the room to close
windows against the rain,
listen for the breathing
of a baby boy who slept
curled like a chubby grub
in his snap-up pajamas.

Years later when he stops by,
he knocks on the front door,
a formality that makes me sad.
He strides into our house
like a buccaneer highly tattooed
and smelling of smoke.
When he tells us about the customer
he soothed, friends we've never met,
we're spellbound by the fullness
of his life lived elsewhere.

I remember him as a toddler
escaping the bars of his crib,
a grid of moonlit shadows on the wall.
I feel him climbing back to me.
The vines of my arms wrap
around him; we ride the rocking
chair back to stories where
he found lost treasure
and traveled on a train to the stars.

AT THE EDGES

In the past, both real and imagined, my son and I are standing in western South Dakota where around and behind us a mixed-grass prairie golden dun color, and above us a cloudless iron blue sky. I am rosy with an almost burn and he, a tall child squinting with the light in his dark eyes, has turned mahogany in the month of August. Before school and schedules lay daily claim we travel. A tent in the car means we set up camp easily here and there unfurling blue nylon to stake a home like nomads in the wind. I am from around here where someone who knows someone I know or used to know or am related to can be discovered in small towns. People who eye us are mostly kind or quiet. I don't know what it is like to be Lakota and lose land and a way of life. I don't know what it is like to lose one mother and find another. I want us to be mother and son traveling alone together where at night we see the star fields of white flowers and the way the moon edges toward whole. Sometimes he cries in the car. The adoption counselor said grief is a reservoir to drink from or something like that. When we walk to the trailhead carrying old Army canteens we hear the insect hum and persistent wind through wheatgrass, green needlegrass, blue grama, scarlet globemallow and prairie coneflower. We startle at a rush of grouse flushed by hunters. My son says he doesn't ever want to shoot a gun. He likes it here, and if he says that just to please me, it means he wants to please me and I am pleased. He speaks backpack now, and GPS, guidebook, campsite, poke-and-plumb towns, MPG, gravel roads, First Nations' rights, national wetlands, leave-no-trace, constellations, and morning star. In the litany of language the more we name the more we are.

ANOTHER DAY OF BEING WHITE
[COMING FROM THERE]

I come from dirt. From blown off the plains dirt
that gritted in teeth. I come from places far

away, hungry places where my people ate
turnips and onions. I come from a sexton who rang

the bell in a Swedish town, and a farm laborer
in Poland at a time the borders kept changing.

I come from the pale mash of potatoes,
from men who drank and women who didn't.

From peasants who tried to better themselves,
save money, who went places by ships

and wagons and trains to try their luck in a new
country because the old one squeezed them and

the new one hoped them. I come from dirt. From
the patch where I grew strawberries and buried

bones of little pets. I come from a town
of white people and one Indian artist, a professor

whose shy daughter was beautiful and maybe lonely.
I never talked to her. I come from parents

who crossed over from being land workers
to book readers and teachers, homeowners

with things of value to pass on to their children.
I come from strife and from striving. From

free people as far back as ancestry.com can go.
I come from serious people who didn't laugh

as much as they studied. I come from then and there.
And where am I going, having changed the color

of my family, passing on whatever I can
to my handsome sons, and where will they go,

what tracks on earth will they follow?

SUMMONING MY DEAD MOTHER

How assured she sits at my Formica table
eating crusty bread as if it's normal
for the dead to be hungry.
She requests toast and honey
unlike her usual oatmeal.
Honey, she calls me, *sometimes
I like a change. Routine is boring.*

Clinking down her cup of coffee
she takes pitch-black and so scalding
you'd think it'd strip the skin
of her tongue raw, *Catch me up,*
she says knowing I haven't talked
to anyone for three days.

I'm wearing her old bathrobe
with big pink roses
and a food stain.
She doesn't appear to notice
she's insubstantial as wind
that stirs a willow tree
washing its long hair in lake water
and blooming for the bees.

SUPP-HOSE

The tough stockings for her purple varicose veins
   rarely got runs.
If one did, my mother gave it the job of binding wounds
in tree trunks chewed by rabbits.
The color she bought for her skin tone
was called *flesh* back before industry cared about variety.

Mother hooked the compression stockings high
on her panty girdle hose supports.
(Don't garter snaps sound like something to eat?)
When she unhooked her nylons,
the back and front of her thighs
were stamped with red marks.

Oh Mother, years later I commiserate with you
living through hot Dakota summers
in those long dresses and huggy lingerie.
Remember how the girls in our household
peeled off sweat-soaked underwear at dusk
and sat outside in muumuus patterned with exotic flowers?
I want to tell you that two of your daughters
had their veins stripped in a procedure
   I get woozy thinking about.

When I take a bath, I think how you liked a long soak.
On your towel bars hung to dry, a week's worth
of beige-colored Supp-hose.
Warm water helps our throbbing, doesn't it?
I still buy Epsom salt for soothing body and soul.

LAUNDROMAT

I carried a cargo of my clothing
to the Do-It-Yourself Laundry—
free parking, clean floors, well lit.
Workaday women flushed with heat
loaned bleach or broke bills
to buy detergent from the coin-op.

Lulled by churning sounds
we waited on plastic chairs
for timers to beep, reading
ragged magazines about diets
and disasters of famous people.
Wet garments pressed to the windows
of washing machines like ghosts in the rain.

Once I watched a woman in a housedress
fold a tower of her family's underwear:
a man's big boxers, a child's briefs,
baby diapers, and her ultra-white panties.
Hip-bumping the door open, both hands
on her basket, she suddenly twirled
like a dancer.

Now I own my own washer and dryer,
I do the job alone.
Today I drove by the laundromat
thinking of the women inside, bone-tired
with their piles of clothing and their patience.
Steam silvered the window and exhaust
billowed clean against the bluing sky.

A BABY SHOWER NEAR THE END OF THE WORLD

The women looked out from the windows of a tall building at an ocean that had remembered how much land it used to own. Over time water rose and leaked into almost every corner on earth. The women had come in rowboats and tied them to balconies on the fourth floor. From high up, the fleet looked like elm leaves. Since the elevator had long since sizzled and shut down, the women climbed ten flights of stairs to their friend's apartment, pausing on the landings to catch their breath. The athletic ones encouraged others: *Keep going! Good luck! You're almost there!* Luck was something everyone was running out of. Although food was scarce, the hostess had come up with canned ingredients to make cold soup. Gifts for the baby girl were hand-me-downs: red rattle, knit bonnet, and five plastic bibs. The new mother was grateful for everything, trying to smile as her eyes grew gray with tears. Each woman took a long turn holding the baby to peer into the universe in her bright eyes and take in her smell of spring and the beginning of everything.

ANOTHER DAY OF BEING WHITE
[MISS MARY]

No matter how often
she addressed me as Miss Margaret
I refused to call her Miss Mary,
used only her sweet first name,
the practice in my circles
for people friendly
and casual with each other.

You'd think only the young
would be heedless as I was
of her implied wish.
Though the same middle age,
we weren't the same color.

Having marched to free women
from labels advertising
their marital status to men
and prospective employers,
I signed on for Ms. or nothing,
didn't back down when I should
have yielded to her history.

If I tell you she never scolded me
and once held my hand when
I was blue, you will know
something about her dignity
and something about the depth
of my regret now, years later,
for refusing her a word
she graciously conferred on me.

PLACE SETTINGS

Spoons and forks crowd drawers,
more tableware than ever needed.
Nowadays the pandemic makes it
just two of us for meals.
Not even face-to-face across the table
we eat by the TV
drawn into currents of disaster.

The table where we don't eat
is wide oak, has many leaves.
From frequent use of Pledge,
lemon lingers in the dining room.

A dozen chairs fit around, easy.
Decorated with flowers, cloth napkins,
laden with food, the table
with its many legs has been
a caravan of conversation and closeness.
These days I use it to fold clothes.

Last January when the table was full,
everyone took turns telling
what they hoped for the new year—
weddings, travel, other joys
that didn't get to happen.
That night we turned off lights
for a birthday cake's chorus of candles.
During the long in-breath of wishing
the circle of dear faces was lit
before the tiny flames were blown out
and the faces disappeared.

DURING THE LONG STAY-AT-HOME

Doesn't everyone first frame
the puzzle picture by finding the edges?

Each piece on the table resembles
a little country, its borders

formed by a snaking river, war
or surveyors' calculation.

So many uneven bits to eye
or jockey into empty spaces.

Based on size, color, striation,
or what-the-heck good luck

we tuck one or two into place
each time we pass the table

with the box cover propped up
to show us a future

where life is whole again,
red flowers blooming on a trellis,

birds free to congregate
and fly whenever they wish.

MASKED

People go out half-faced.
We don't get frowns or smiles.
I miss pearly pink
and Goth brown lipstick
worn by the daughters of my friends.
I miss the daughters of my friends.

Toothy surprises stay hidden:
braces, also the gold incisor
with a dollar sign in the mouth
of my student in prison.
I miss my student.

We focus on features we see:
a forehead registering excitement
or anger on a stretch of skin
smooth as Saran Wrap
or aged by divots of worry.
There's a lot to worry about.

Each half-a-face human has eyes.
Color will someday bloom in the irises
when we will be close enough
to see through the beautiful apertures
into the soul.

CAN I BE FORGIVEN

for how well
the past year fit me
with its elastic time
and deep pockets
of privacy?
Each day I wore
the blue dress of solitude
joy entered me
like yellow light
through wheat fields.

HANAMI

Blight damaged
my neighbor's cherry trees.
She prunes branches
and dry infected berries
known as mummies.

The knotted trees live on,
descendants of slim cultivars
Tokyo's mayor presented
our country's capital
more than 100 years ago.
Each spring a pink paper chain
flourishes along the tidal basin.

In a haiku about cherry blossoms,
Basho writes: *how many many things they call to mind.*

What comes to my mind
is how after Pearl Harbor,
angry white Americans
hacked branches and trunks
of blameless cherry trees,
dragged some away like hostages.
In the current pandemic
they are taking it out against
bodies of Asian Americans.

Hanami is the Japanese word
for peaceful flower gazing.
The sun taps lightly
on a purple crocus and it opens.
When their season passes
cherry blossoms will fall, laying
a soft blanket on the grass.

PASSING STORM

—Inspired by Passing Storm,
a painting by Margaret Lockwood

The squall releases its darkness
to a blush of low clouds and gold on high,
a tumult calming.

It's like dawn when new colors appear.
In the weft of waves to the far horizon,
greens meld with shades
of ink, slate, and brighter blues
to make liquid turquoise.
There's mystery in the whisper of mauve.

The last four years pummeled us.
To be with this painting feels hopeful
we have passed through the worst
of our country's tempest.

Gone the grumble of thunder,
smell of ozone, white veins of lightning.
Runnels of rain no longer slant across the sky.
Winds that beat the long, wide body
of water have tamed.
Rough rubble on the lake's surface
subsides to stippled ripples.
Clouds break up; the overcast is clearing.

We watch for pure blue,
breathe the green fragrance
of after-rain, want to believe
as our ancestors did
that it will cleanse and protect us.

ANOTHER DAY OF BEING WHITE
[WHITE MATTER]

*—White objects fully reflect and scatter all the visible
wavelengths of light,* according to Wikipedia

The white of parchment and book pages,
bleached flour and powdered sugar,

the sugar of divinity candy that makes teeth ache.
The white of toothpaste for wilder

wide-open smiles, the white of skin scream, no—
skin cream, the itch of bleach

for people passing one degree lighter,
the albino squirrel disappearing

in snowfall, snow geese on an icy lake,
a wedding cake, onions and rice,

white lines on asphalt, the white-man-walking
figure on a traffic signal (followed

by the warning of a red raised hand).
Whiteout in the mountain camp, bedsheets,

Klan robes and cone-hat evil, white
in the gray of Stone Mountain, eons

and ache of blooming cotton bolls'
fibrous white harvest, slim wafers

of God's body at communion, heat from
waxed candles upbraiding the cathedral air.

Prettied up in name and painted on a wall,
it's White Dover, Cloud 9, Chantilly Lace.

The winter fur of snowshoe hares, childhood
chalk marked on blackboards, and white

headlights dimmed for the drive-in movie theater
to see big faces on a white screen.

Fancy panties in a store, white gowns for doctors,
white gloves of propriety, whites of our eyes

to be fired upon, white heat, white noise, white
outline marking a Black body where it fell.

Also white lies, whitewash, White House.

ANOTHER DAY OF BEING WHITE
[TERMINOLOGY]

My mouth stumbles on the latest terms—
    do I pronounce *Latinx* right?

I balk at using *queer* even though it's on T-shirts
    at *gay* pride events.
I'm old enough to remember my high school friend taking
    the double-barreled hit of "you *queer faggot*"
    screamed from a passing car.
A sloe gin bottle smashed on the sidewalk near us.

Ms. was revolutionary back then.
We've come a long way, *baby*!
(I can use *baby* for women, but men can't,
    although everyone uses *ladies* at tennis.)

I donate to the United Negro College Fund
    and the NAACP, yet don't feel at home
    saying *Negro* or *colored people,*
    but *people of color* seems OK for now.
Words the current U.S. Census offers
    are *African American* or *Black.*
Ralph Ellison was never comfortable with *Black,* although
    he and his circle of friends were certainly beautiful.

Canada doesn't collect data on race.
Some people call my son *mixed,*
    a word that makes me think: breed of dogs.
When pressed to assign him a racial category, I say
    biracial, although race is not biology,
    but a social construct.

When he was little, my son grew upset
    with the inaccuracy of my self-attribution: *white*.
"You are *pink! Pink!*" he insisted (he who is now a *they*),
    then picked a piggy pink crayon to color me
    in his family drawing.
Pinko is sometimes still used to disparage someone
    with socialist leanings.
My exacting son claims *brown* for himself, not *Black*.

When he was a baby, his *white* great-grandmother,
    101 years old, asked to hold "the *pickaninny*."
Each time we visited, she believed his complexion
    was getting lighter as if I rubbed off on him in that way.
I had a terrible dream I'm like her, in a nursing home
    with a pissy smell.
I'm aged and addled.
When my son visits, I find his darkness
    foreign and frightening.
Up from a child's counting rhyme comes an old slurry name
    for someone who looks like him:
        Eenie, meanie, miney, mo . . .
This is my nightmare, and it might be his, too.

FOR THE TIME BEING

I don't know where the world got to
that time when the baby was little
and I was its blurry-tired mother,
when I left my body on the lakeshore,
in a stretch of grass and rose
as if mist toward the clouds.
It wasn't like being taken up in rapture
by a majestic god, more like a giant animal
carried me carefully in its maw.
I was its furry young it did not spit out.
I trusted its presence, that I'd be returned
to the wet beach towel and dry heat.
Shrill voices of children sounded
in the distance. None was my child.
All that was going on—the games,
splashing, a sharp shout—
asked nothing of me.
For the time being I was happy
as someone with no obligations
drowsing while light flowed
over my face and closed eyelids.
Red radiated in my vision, perhaps
the sun or the shadow of my blood.

INSTRUMENTS

Our house stands close to the neighbor's house.
From my living room I hear Josie
next door on her clarinet.
I tense as she plays Cole Porter's "I Love You"
but today she hits every note.
My husband looks up from his book
and smiles: *She's getting better*.

Our own grown sons inflicted their green practice
on us and others—one blaring on his trumpet
and the other pounding a repetitive drumbeat
accented by a hi-hat's crash.

Now Josie's done her half hour,
it's quiet enough to hear the backyard song sparrows.
I walk to the city pond for a view of other birds
that pass through this time of year.

From afar, trumpeter swans sound like an orchestra
of fourth graders with new instruments that squawk.
When I get close to our country's largest waterfowl,
I see they are grown-ups, paper white and sleek,
that will take off tomorrow two by two—
like most of us, preferring not to live alone.
Instinct drives them toward food and warmth
in coastal estuaries, navigating by sun and stars
the way sailors once did.

When birds behave as they should and we consider
children who grew through the chaotic noise
of their instruments to make real music of their lives,
the arrangement of life seems orderly and beautiful.

THREE

GOOD LIFE

It's amazing how much goes right with our bodies
most of the time.
We realize this when something goes wrong.

When sand abraded the cornea of one eye,
with my working eye I looked online at illustrations
of the astonishing human eye
with its complex features, chambers and regions.

My doctor called the body a *forgiving animal.*
My whole life has been better than expected.

I'm not tall grass even in a small field of green
yet I'm waving in the wind with others.

The latest tests show no further change
in the condition of my heart,
which was enlarging—a metaphor I like, but it's dangerous.

All my life I have been loved, enough
rain has fallen to grow a garden,
and I receive society and solitude in good proportion.

I've outgrown the crazy binges of girlhood
and learned to stop lying except in poems.

How can I celebrate the life received,
the body that has carried me for years without great cost?

Forego self-improvement, loosen the cinch of plans,
honor the twin gods of patience and peace.
Be a new butterfly on the zinnia, drying its wings.

ANOTHER DAY OF BEING WHITE
[AT THE NAIL SALON]

Black-haired workers in nurse-
white uniforms (USA size 0)
perch on low stools.
They speak their own staccato
behind paper masks,
ask *too hot?*, say *twenty dollars.*
Moving lips make a slight tremor
when they laugh.
Larger women (I am one)
on overstuffed vibrating
chairs present bunioned feet,
toenails like bits of seashell.
Lang Vu employs a pumice
stone, warm towel for drying.
I pick pretty pretty paint
(Strawberry Summer Burst),
sigh with satisfaction.
Workers here grasp
the long tail of an old war.
We get this kind tending.
They get this kind of work.
I tip well out of gratitude?
generosity? guilt? I place
money in the cupped hands
of a young woman
and leave on good feet
in good sandals.
No bombs fall from my sky.
My water's not tainted
by Agent Orange.
My children play in fields
free of unexploded ordnance.

ANNUAL VISIT TO THE OPTOMETRIST

My eyes spill artificial tears making the attentive face
of the optometrist soft and blurry.
Black on the white screen, a capital E
looks like a broken comb.
Uppercase C and G interchange.

Outside the room are sounds of cattle lowing—
no, it's the melded voices of people passing time
in the waiting room, learning to be patient.

And now Dr. Capon—yes, like chicken in French—
begins his singsong admonitions
as if a grade school crossing guard:
look right look left look up look down.
The doctor dilates my pupils to the size of my son's,
moony on marijuana.

Darwin puzzled over how his theory
could explain our magnificent orb of vision:
a patch of light-sensitive cells evolving to separate parts—
lens, retina, pupil.

When I step into the sunlight
wearing huge free plastic shades,
pain and radiance dazzle equally.

SELF-EXAMINATION

Faint pain in her breast
makes her grope herself,
hand under her bra
like a teenage crush,
fingertips probing
soft flesh in a cotton cup.

She feels around
in the labyrinthine process
of self-examination
returning from the center
going outward unwinding
in a circular pattern.

She used to imagine
X-ray eyes of God
locating lies and greed
as she walked silently
on a pilgrim's path
in a spiral of stone
praying to be healthy and good
or at least better at living.

Her fingers stop to probe
a lump and fear leaks
into her chest:
has the disease
of her mother and sister
lurked since birth
casing her body
to plant cells like sins
no doctor can cast out?

RED DRESS

In the back of the attic closet
on a rack of old duds for Goodwill,
a dress still hangs, brief and bright,
pert, a ruby coronation.

A man at a swing dance whispered
You shine in your orbit
as you twirled and the skirt
fanned out to your thighs.
Later you leaned back on a hot car's hood
to drink a long and starry kiss.

In a mirror when you hold the dress
against your figure, its svelte shape
won't stretch to cover you,
wide where you used to be slim.
Parts of you that lifted and were light
are now among fallen things.

You could just keep a swatch
of fabric to pin in a picture frame
with a bit of slippery wedding gown
and a snippet of baby blue flannel.
But you want the memory whole
of being wrapped in the silk
of a red hot damn of a dress.

WITH WALT WHITMAN AT WEIGHT WATCHERS

The new guy with a big belly and Santa beard
sits in the back row. A dented hat. Buttons
on his shirt strain to contain him. At weigh-in
he removed his shoes to balance elephantine
on the scale. His voice is lusty and self-contented
in his poems, but here he slouches, no longer
finding the fat sweet that sticks to his own bones.

He fidgets on a plastic chair unkind to his amplitude.
The group discusses low calorie snacks like rice cakes
and how to resist all you can eat buffets.
Rocking back and forth on the worn seat of his size
XXL pants, he looks expectantly around the room
as if at a party that will soon provide confections.

When he stands to leave, he says it's poetry not lunch
calling his soul, detached, ceaselessly seeking.
Like Pied Piper, he leads us into the weightless air.
We sit in a public park with no gab of gains and losses,
listen to him recite *Song of Myself*.
Breeze is soft on our bodies as if we each wear
a loose blouse of pleasure.

LOTUS

When it begins a body is a bendy thing,
    created to be collapsible.
Think of a baby's birth. Soft spots
    let pieces of skull shift like tectonic plates.
Think how a body softens
    in the hands of a lover.

When I used to meditate, legs crossed,
    eyes closed, my light-filled mind turned
from worry and want—a flower
    giving itself completely to the sun.
My bones seemed to flex and fold,
    agreeable as lawyers
that yield their arguments,
    go home and bake bread.

Now that my leg's been broken
    on purpose, cut apart
and reassembled with a metal knee,
    I can't sit in triangular composure
at yoga, cannot curve
    into the Half Lord of the Fishes posture
nor do a High Lunge.
    But the Happy Baby position
is still mine, happy happy baby
    playing with its toes.

At the end of class I relax
    into *savasana*, my body
flat and face up in a pose of rest,
    a stillness like death.

NIGHT ON THE TOWN

White stars have fallen into the trees
of Rice Park where we can see

the cold statue of F. Scott Fitzgerald
wearing his stocking cap of snow.

Nearby, a silver platter of frozen ice
is etched by many blades.

Skaters are figurines cast against
the granite walls of Landmark Center.

Eight dollars rents two pairs of leather skates.
How long since we last let go, pushed off?

Like unsteady boats, we set out
on a wobbly rink-go-round.

Muscle memory instructs: relax knees
so legs can shove and stroke to glide.

Orbiting like planets, following strangers
in bright coats who also follow us

we blow blue clouds of breath into the night.
Everything whirls: skaters, snowflakes, stars.

MEDICARE BIRTHDAY

How many more times
will I spy that first fat robin
returning in March?

I back my car out of the garage
craning my stiff neck, concerned
about what I can no longer see.

Especially in spring I imagine
letting the car go where it wants,
such as to my first home
above the Missouri River Valley
where wild plum
blooms in the ditches
and tall cottonwoods,
their new leaves glittering,
lean over the cradle of a stream.

AT OUR AGE

When my husband and I walk
gingerly on winter sidewalks
sometimes young people barrel
toward us wearing earbuds,
their body language showing
that we gray ghosts are invisible.

Swerving in slow-mo to the side
as they stampede by, we're baffled
and comment under our breath
about their being clueless,
then plod on again, old skaters
holding hands on ice that will
become more perilous as we go.

AFTER A FALL

With a hand that can't wave
or make a fist, the exclamation
of a long arm isn't dotted.
One mitten, one glove—useless.
A numb bundle at the end of a limb
flaps like a scarecrow.
All writing is invisible ink.

Speak against forgetting
the hand's fan of little bones,
cuticles like crescent moons,
the scar from a rabbit bite,
a ring of friendship,
the extravagance of pink peony
painted on the nails.

When the hand returns,
pale and weak from enclosure,
welcome it like a prodigal child.

Once again the sunflower
of the hand extends toward light.
Seeds can be planted
and patted in the earth.
The hand can explore a face,
raise a toast, gesture OK,
meet its mate in applause.

Oh, to feel a dog's rough
tongue on fingertips,
to tease a button through
a very small hole.

GROWING WILD IN COOK COUNTY IN JULY

Ping by plop, raspberries pile up
in a steel bucket.
Cup by cup and slow hot hours
of mosquito-buzzed patience,
the bucket is heaped.

Later, the gathered harvest
is washed and laid to dry
on paper towels—
red forest fruit, an errant insect,
a single leaf.

Picked through and placed in a pan
with brief heat, the hollow
hallowed berries soften to be pressed
through a colander
to smooth gel.

Now strut a dozen glass jars
topped by silver lids,
curved bellies bursting
with scarlet wonder
ready to store.

When the weather turns cold
and the radio coughs bad news,
a swirl of raspberry jam
on toasted bread dials the day
back to summer.

FIRE EATERS

Raw meat, beans, onions with their Saturnalian rings,
tomatoes in their Buddha-body opulence

wait for the blazing cook, apron stained
blood-red pepper and cumin gold.

It's said that a ghost chili grows in Madagascar
so pungent it can kill outright.

If you live, your lifespan lengthens.
You will enjoy sexual power to the end of your days.

High on the Scoville scale of heat,
chili powder from Hatch, New Mexico,

bronze as earth, smells spicy enough
to blast a hole in the cheek.

A bowl of capsaicin-rich food ignites
a furnace flame and crackle in your flesh.

You're ash that returns as a firebird.
You dance to a salsa kick of music.

Makes you feel like poetry—
the top of your head taken off.

Hot! Hotsy-totsy.
Makes you want more.

LITTLE DOMESTIC DANCE

In this series of gray days
        and seasonal hubbub
a night alone just us,
        we almost blow it
by an argument about a birthday card
        so silly it's hard to relate.
You whack whiskers
        from scallions and I slam
salmon into cold water.
        We stand with backs to each other.
The pan warms oil into amber.
        The smell of garlic . . .
A cock's comb of red tomato . . .
        Bread to cut with a toothy knife . . .
You stir risotto, spoon a dab:
        here, you try it, too.
Our faces ruddy with heat
        we bounce to the beat
of Beyoncé's "Crazy in Love."

AUBADE IN JANUARY, WITH CARDINALS

Shovel the driveway, salt the ice.
I roll like a wave to your side
of the bed, against your back
with its archipelago of bones.

Friends send pictures of themselves
standing by tumbleweeds in Texas,
lolling on a beach blanket in Florida,
wide smiles lit from within
like jack-o'-lanterns.

We mate for life and do not migrate,
live by the great clock
that appears earlier each day.
Weather will change its cold ways:
hepatica's purple bloom up
through patches of melting snow.

This morning we watch a male cardinal
with his punk hairdo crest
place a black sunflower seed
in his mate's mouth the way
we might feed each other dark chocolate.
Sweet-sweet-sweet calls the cardinal.

STROKE

It was a mild one, they say I'm lucky,
my husband tells me over the phone.

It was only yesterday he saw
everything doubled—
a book, his finger, my face.
Was the trouble his tired eyes?
A call line nurse urged Emergency.

I drove him to the hospital's red door,
no farther. COVID: no visitors.

All night alone in our bed
built for two, I tried to hush
the insistent insomniac of worry.
Would my husband walk again,
talk, know who I am?

The MRI image of his beautiful brain
showed a small region gone dark forever.
What memories might be lost?
Jokes that made his students laugh?
The first meal we ate together?
Our son's favorite tune on his trumpet?

This morning my husband aced
cognitive tests, counting down
from one hundred by sevens,

making a long list of common words
that begin with the letter m:
morning
music
mountain
mystery
moon
more . . .

GETTING THE CONTINENTAL DRIFT

In the shade of a tree
my husband still in his pj's
takes a geology course on his iPad.

He tells me there's great unrest
in the mountains; rock
we think unyielding actually flows.
Under the Earth's crust
gigantic tectonic plates
shift and shove.

In grade school
continents were displayed
like the peeling of a flattened orange
on a map of Earth.
Even a schoolchild could see
that land masses looked pulled
apart from one another.
I'd imagine moving Africa,
a puzzle piece, to snuggle its western coastline
into eastern South America.

And they are still moving, my husband says.
Someday Africa will smash into Europe
as Australia migrates north.
250 million years from now
one huge landmass, the Pangea Ultima,
will form from this flux and flow.

We continue discussing the Earth's thrash,
its bronco of energy, mantel and sub-layers.

He stands up a little wobbly
on his new knee and touches my hair.
On solid ground before, now I feel
the Earth move under my feet.

SPRING AUBADE IN BLUE

—Inspired by Finding Rest,
a painting by Margaret Lockwood

Stay still beyond dawn's bluing,
laved in a bath of soft light.
Lie in the harboring arms, beloved,
half-dreaming of warm water and birds.

Softly, bare light bathes us.
Breeze teases breath in and out of curtains.
We're half-dreaming water and birds:
new world warblers, yellow and blue.

Breeze teases breath from still curtains.
Our restless nature disturbs us.
The new world warblers, yellow and blue,
unfurl the sails of their busy song.

Our restless nature seeks to stir us.
Why not, when we need respite,
drop the sails of our busy lives?
Drift with me still beyond dawn's bluing.

AUDUBON'S *THE BIRDS OF AMERICA*, COLOR-PLATE 211

If you, too, dream to be born again
as a bird, wouldn't you want to be
a great blue heron, rare vagrant
wintering in the Azores and coastal Spain,
snacking on shrimp while wading
on long, beautiful legs? And if

you loved your life as a human who
sheltered in a small house by a lake, you
could summer there again, nesting
in the white pine, fishing on the shore
in the blue Zen of stillness when early
morning ambers the eastern sky.

INDEX OF TITLES

AUTHOR'S GRATITUDE

Poets, both dead and living, continually remind me of the necessity and pleasures of poetry. As I was working on these poems, I found encouragement in the words of poet James Wright: "The most powerfully subversive force in this country is poetry, but by poetry I don't mean a scheme of metrics, I mean a realization that one's own life is irrevocably precious." Insightful input and support from the Onionskins group strengthened my poems. Donna Isaac, the first reader of a rough draft, gave the book and me a lift. David Grothe, Joan Johnson, and Connie Wanek were proofreading and copy editing angels who went above and beyond in their care and kindness. However, if there are errors in the poems, hold me responsible! Heartfelt thank-yous to Norton Stillman and John Toren, Nodin Press colleagues who have become dear friends. My husband, sons, and siblings could not be more accepting and supportive of me as a writer of poems in which they may have a stake. As one of my sons said after reading a poem in which a son appears: "This is art and your truth at the time you wrote it. I get that."

photo: David Grothe

ABOUT THE AUTHOR

Margaret Hasse lives and works in the Twin Cities of Minnesota. *Summoned* is her sixth full-length collection of poetry. A collaboration with watercolor artist Sharon DeMark early in the COVID-19 pandemic resulted in *Shelter*, a book of poems and paintings about places of refuge. Hasse has been an editor of two anthologies, most recently *Rocked by the Waters: Poems of Motherhood*, with Athena Kildegaard. *The Call of Glacier Park*, a chapbook, is forthcoming in 2022. For her poetry, Hasse has received fellowships and awards from the National Endowment for the Arts, Minnesota State Arts Board, McKnight Foundation through The Loft Literary Center, Jerome Foundation, and the Midwest and the National Independent Publishers Associations. To learn more, visit margarethasse.com or poetryfoundation.org.